# FIRST FACTS ABOUT
# PREHISTORIC ANIMALS

Written by Gina Phillips

Illustrated by F.S. Persico

**Incorporated**

Copyright © 1991 by Kidsbooks Inc.
7004 N. California Ave.
Chicago, IL 60645

Prehistoric backboned animals came in many different shapes and sizes. They walked on land, swam in the sea, and flew in the air. Beginning as tiny sea creatures, they developed over many millions of years into fish, reptiles, dinosaurs, birds, and mammals.

**Stegosaurus**
(steg-uh-SAWR-us)

**Stegosaurus** was a peaceful plant eater who lived in North America about 150 million years ago. Its body was the size of an elephant, but it was about 30 feet from its nose to the tip of its tail. Stegosaurus had a very small head—only 16 inches long—and a tiny brain the size of a Ping-Pong ball.

No one knows for certain the purpose of the row of plates that ran down the back of Stegosaurus. Some scientists think the plates were used to help control the animal's body temperature. Others suggest the plates may have been used for defense. Stegosaurus's tail had four large spikes, which may also have been used to help defend it from large enemies like **Allosaurus.**

Allosaurus stood 16½ feet tall on strong hind legs that were good for running after prey. Fearsome, flesh-eating Allosaurus had a huge head. Its powerful jaws had sharp, daggerlike teeth that were 2 to 4 inches long.

**Allosaurus**
(AL-uh-SAWR-us)

3

**Brachiosaurus** weighed more than 10 elephants—
up to 160,000 pounds. This huge plant eater was one of
the largest land animals that ever lived.

Using its long neck, it was able to munch leaves
on the tops of 40-foot trees. Its nostrils were located
in a bump on top of its head, which led scientists to believe that this massive
dinosaur lived in water. We now know this is not true. A more likely explanation
for the placement of the nostrils is that they allowed Brachiosaurus to breathe
while its mouth was underwater feeding. Brachiosaurus roamed the warm
forests of river plains on its big padded feet. Remains of this reptile have
been found in the western United States, Africa,
and Europe.

**Diplodocus** lived in the western part of the United States at the same time as Brachiosaurus. Smaller and lighter than Brachiosaurus, Diplodocus was much longer. A complete skeleton of Diplodocus has been found. It is the longest dinosaur skeleton known. The body is only 19 feet long, but it has a 26-foot-long neck and a 45-foot-long whiplike tail—a total of 90 feet. Diplodocus means "double beam," referring to the Y-shaped spines on its backbone.

Diplodocus probably moved very slowly on its stout but strong legs. It may have lived in herds, which would have given it some protection from flesh eaters. Diplodocus had thin, pencil-shaped teeth located in the front of its mouth, and probably swallowed pebbles and stones to help digest its food.

**Diplodocus**
(dih-PLOD-uh-kus)

**Brachiosaurus**
(brake-ee-uh-SAWR-us)

5

Ichthyosaurus was a prehistoric sea reptile shaped like a dolphin. It lived at the same time as the dinosaurs but was not related to them. This "fish lizard" measured anywhere from 8 to 30 feet long. Ichthyosaurus was a powerful swimmer. Four paddlelike limbs steered its streamlined body as it sped through the water. It ate fish, squid, and shellfish, which it crushed in its long, pointed jaws. Unable to go ashore to build a nest, it gave birth to live young in the water.

Ichthyosaurus swam in the warm oceans that once covered most of the western part of the United States. Remains have also been found in South America and Europe.

**Elasmosaurus**
(ee-LAZ-muh-SAWR-us)

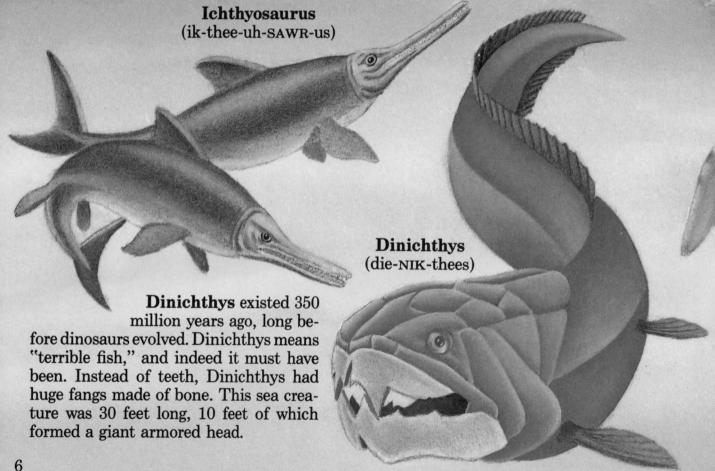

**Ichthyosaurus**
(ik-thee-uh-SAWR-us)

**Dinichthys**
(die-NIK-thees)

**Dinichthys** existed 350 million years ago, long before dinosaurs evolved. Dinichthys means "terrible fish," and indeed it must have been. Instead of teeth, Dinichthys had huge fangs made of bone. This sea creature was 30 feet long, 10 feet of which formed a giant armored head.

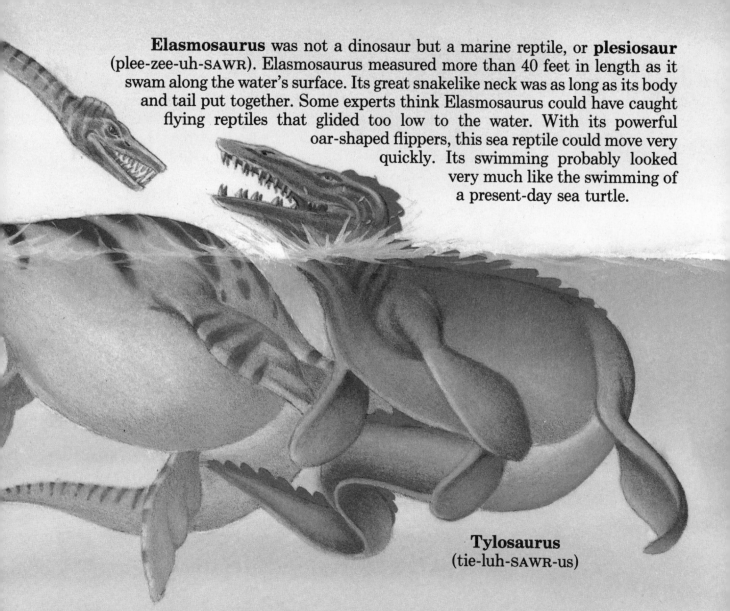

**Elasmosaurus** was not a dinosaur but a marine reptile, or **plesiosaur** (plee-zee-uh-SAWR). Elasmosaurus measured more than 40 feet in length as it swam along the water's surface. Its great snakelike neck was as long as its body and tail put together. Some experts think Elasmosaurus could have caught flying reptiles that glided too low to the water. With its powerful oar-shaped flippers, this sea reptile could move very quickly. Its swimming probably looked very much like the swimming of a present-day sea turtle.

**Tylosaurus**
(tie-luh-SAWR-us)

**Tylosaurus** was a 50-foot-long marine lizard that lived 75 to 100 million years ago. Its huge mouth had many sharp, cone-shaped teeth. The teeth suggest this animal fed mainly on other sea reptiles and fish. Tylosaurus was capable of killing fish weighing many hundreds of pounds.

Tylosaurus fossils have been found in Kansas and northern Europe.

The "armored lizard," **ankylosaur** (an-kee-luh-SAWR), came in many sizes. The largest was as big as a bus and weighed 8,000 pounds. The smallest was the size of a human. These plant-eating creatures were truly the "tanks" of the dinosaur world.

Of all the ankylosaurs, **Palaeoscincus** probably had the best protection from its enemies. Its entire upper side was covered with bony plates. A row of short spikes stuck out on each side of its body and tail. The tail, with a knob on the end, could be swung like a club.

Palaeoscincus could likely be killed only by a flesh eater both strong enough and smart enough to turn it over to expose its soft underbelly.

Ankylosaurs were one of the last dinosaurs to die out. Fossils have been found in Montana, western Canada, and Asia.

**Ornithomimus** is the best known of the "ostrich dinosaurs." It ate fruit, small animals, and the eggs of other dinosaurs. It had a horny, toothless beak and looked a little like today's ostrich.

Using its strong hind legs, this reptile was able to run very fast. Ornithomimus used its speed to catch prey and to escape from enemies. This 8-foot-tall animal had a relatively large brain and was probably one of the more intelligent dinosaurs.

Fossils have been found in the western United States and in Tibet.

**Ornithomimus**
(or-nith-uh-MEE-mus)

**Palaeoscincus**
(pay-lee-o-SINK-us)

9

**Dromaeosaurus** means "swift lizard." This fast, fierce flesh-eating hunter ran upright on powerful hind legs. Its long, stiff tail was needed for balance. Each foot had a razor-sharp 3-inch claw that was used to slash and tear apart prey. These claws had side-to-side movement, making them very dangerous. When running, Dromaeosaurus held these claws in an upright position to keep them out of the way. This 6-foot-tall dinosaur weighed about 100 pounds and had a large brain for its size.

**Dromaeosaurus**
(drom-ee-uh-SAWR-us)

Dromaeosaurus used its great speed to hunt small animals and may have formed packs to hunt large plant-eating dinosaurs. A possible victim could have been **Corythosaurus** or "helmet lizard." This 33-foot-long duck-billed dinosaur weighed 2 to 3 tons.

Fossils of both of these dinosaurs have been found in western Canada.

**Corythosaurus**
(CO-RITH-a-SAWR-us)

While dinosaurs roamed the land, flying lizards known as **pterosaurs** (tair-uh-SAWRS) ruled the prehistoric skies. These unusual reptiles had bodies that were covered with fur. They may have been warm-blooded and very likely cared for their young, as do present day birds.

   **Quetzalcoatlus**, discovered in Texas in the 1970s, is the largest known pterosaur. Its 150 pound body was carried along by huge wings that spanned 35 to 40 feet. Quetzalcoatlus was the size of a small airplane and probably needed only a slight breeze to lift off the ground.

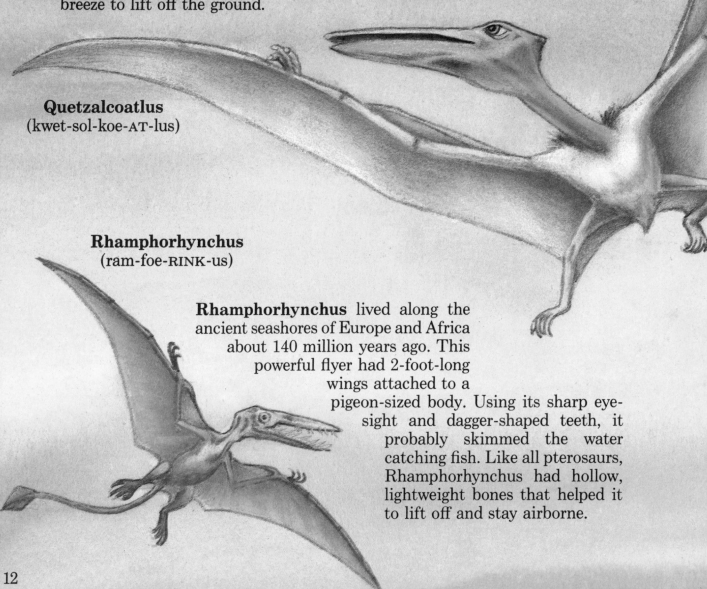

**Quetzalcoatlus**
(kwet-sol-koe-AT-lus)

**Rhamphorhynchus**
(ram-foe-RINK-us)

**Rhamphorhynchus** lived along the ancient seashores of Europe and Africa about 140 million years ago. This powerful flyer had 2-foot-long wings attached to a pigeon-sized body. Using its sharp eyesight and dagger-shaped teeth, it probably skimmed the water catching fish. Like all pterosaurs, Rhamphorhynchus had hollow, lightweight bones that helped it to lift off and stay airborne.

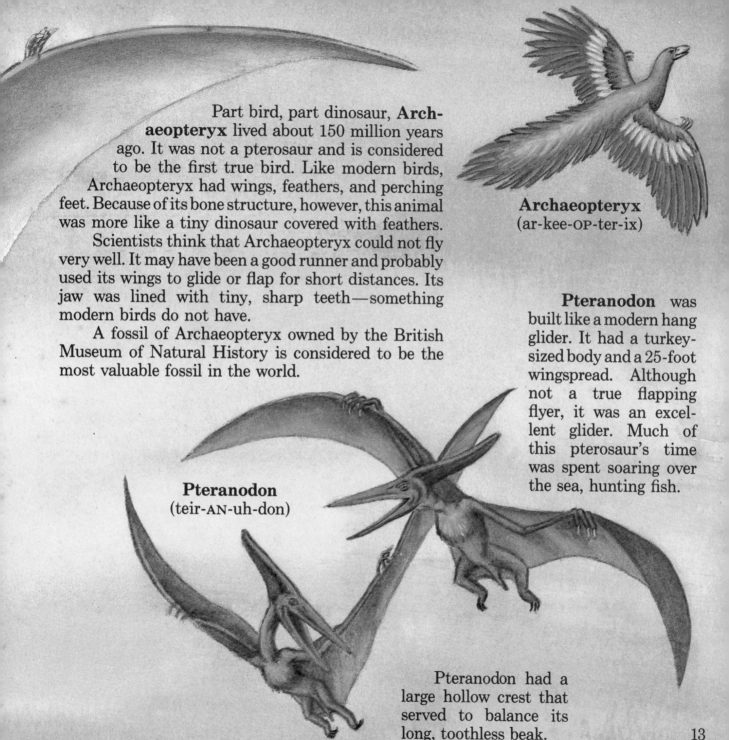

Part bird, part dinosaur, **Archaeopteryx** lived about 150 million years ago. It was not a pterosaur and is considered to be the first true bird. Like modern birds, Archaeopteryx had wings, feathers, and perching feet. Because of its bone structure, however, this animal was more like a tiny dinosaur covered with feathers.

Scientists think that Archaeopteryx could not fly very well. It may have been a good runner and probably used its wings to glide or flap for short distances. Its jaw was lined with tiny, sharp teeth—something modern birds do not have.

A fossil of Archaeopteryx owned by the British Museum of Natural History is considered to be the most valuable fossil in the world.

**Archaeopteryx**
(ar-kee-OP-ter-ix)

**Pteranodon** was built like a modern hang glider. It had a turkey-sized body and a 25-foot wingspread. Although not a true flapping flyer, it was an excellent glider. Much of this pterosaur's time was spent soaring over the sea, hunting fish.

**Pteranodon**
(teir-AN-uh-don)

Pteranodon had a large hollow crest that served to balance its long, toothless beak.

13

**Maiasaura**
(mah-ee-ah-SAWR-ah)

14

In 1978, in Montana, a rare and important discovery was made. The remains of an adult duck-billed dinosaur that lived 70 to 80 million years ago were found. Close by was a fossilized nest containing the remains of 15 young dinosaurs. Since the adult was so near, it was presumed to be the mother. This dinosaur was named **Maiasaura,** which means "good mother lizard." Most reptiles do not care for their young and leave them to fend for themselves as soon as they are hatched. The Maiasaura discovery was proof that at least some dinosaurs stayed with and cared for their young. The adult Maiasaura was 30 feet long and stood 15 feet high on its strong hind legs.

Scientists know the 3-foot-long remains of the babies found in the nest were at least one month old. Their teeth showed signs of wear. This meant they were already eating tough or gritty plants.

Newborn babies that were only 18 inches long have also been found in fossilized nests. One nest was 7 feet across and the eggs were arranged in layers. In each layer the eggs were placed in a perfect circle. Many other bowl-shaped nests were found in the same area.

**Parasaurolophus** was a duck-billed dinosaur that stood about 16 feet tall. It was 30 feet long and weighed 3 or 4 tons. On top of its head was a long bony crest. The purpose of the crest is not known. Some experts think the crest may have been used like a trumpet to produce loud sounds. Other scientists think the crest helped the animal's sense of smell. A good sense of smell would have been useful since this plant eater had little other defense against such meat eaters as **Tyrannosaurus.**

**Parasaurolophus**
(par-uh-sawr-OL-uh-fus)

Tyrannosaurus was among the last of the giant meat eaters. The "tyrant lizard" appeared toward the end of the dinosaur era, about 65 million years ago. It was the largest flesh-eating creature ever to walk the earth.

Tyrannosaurus's massive head was almost 5 feet long. Its huge jaws were filled with sharp, curved teeth. Some of these teeth were as long as six inches. This dinosaur walked on two powerful hind legs, using its large tail for balance. The 8-inch claws on its birdlike hind feet were perfect for ripping into its prey. The arms of Tyrannosaurus were so short they could not even reach its mouth.

At a length of 40 feet and weighing 7 tons, Tyrannosaurus could easily terrorize the North American plant eaters of its time.

**Tyrannosaurus**
(tie-RAN-uh-SAWR-us)

**Iguanodon** was the first dinosaur ever discovered and one of the best known. Iguanodon fossils have been found in Europe, North Africa and Asia.

This 10,000-pound dinosaur lived about 120 million years ago. It stood 16 feet high on its hind legs and could munch on the leaves of tall trees. It could also drop down on all fours in order to eat low-growing plants. Iguanodon's spikelike "thumbs" may have been used for defense. It could also run from danger by using its strong legs.

The remains of several Iguanodons have been found together. Scientists think this dinosaur may have traveled in herds, keeping the young in the middle for protection.

**Iguanodon**
(i-GWAN-uh-don)

**Triceratops** was one of the last dinosaurs to become extinct. Its name means "three-horned face." Two of its 3 horns were 40 inches long. It had a bony shield, called a frill, behind its head. Weighing 5 tons, Triceratops was the size of a small truck. Scientists know this reptile was very aggressive because horn scars have been found on many fossils of the frills. Nevertheless, it probably had few enemies. In groups or alone, this well-armed dinosaur could resist any hunter, even Tyrannosaurus.

This four-legged plant eater lived in herds on the open plains. For five million years, great numbers of Triceratops existed in the western part of the United States and Canada. Then, suddenly, Triceratops and other remaining dinosaurs died out.

The mystery of why and how dinosaurs disappeared has still not been solved.

**Triceratops**
(tri-SAIR-uh-tops)

About 65 million years ago the dinosaurs and sea reptiles that had ruled the earth for 120 million years were suddenly gone. In the sea some reptiles survived. On land there were small insect-eating mammals and some birds. Now the time was right for other animals to take over the world.

One of the first new animals was a giant meat-eating bird called **Diatryma.** This prehistoric bird was more than 9 feet tall. It had a very large head and a huge beak. Diatryma could not fly, but it could run with great speed. It was among the largest, fastest, and most feared animals of its time.

Diatryma may have been able to catch and feed on a primitive horse called **Hyracotherium.** Hyracotherium lived in herds. These horses were only the size of foxes and had large toes instead of hooves. Hyracotherium had four toes on its front feet and three toes on the back. These toes helped it to run on the soft ground.

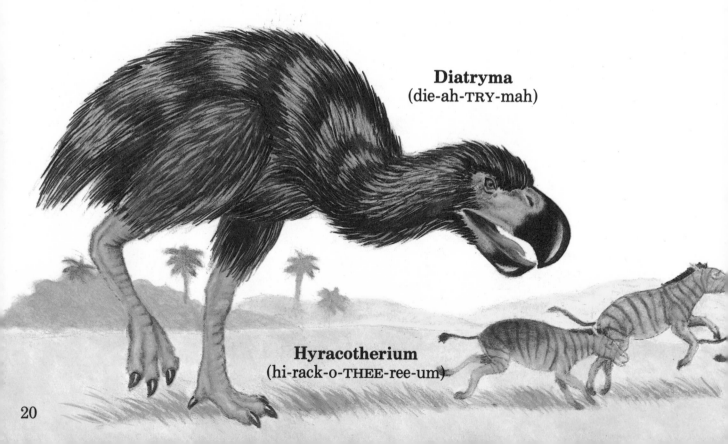

**Diatryma**
(die-ah-TRY-mah)

**Hyracotherium**
(hi-rack-o-THEE-ree-um)

One of the earliest giant prehistoric mammals was **Uintatherium.** This creature was 12 feet long and 7 feet high at the shoulder. Three pairs of short bony horns grew on its head. Although Uintatherium had fangs growing down from its lower jaw, it was a plant eater.

Fifty million years ago, Uintatherium was probably the largest land animal that existed.

**Uintatherium**
(yew-in-ta-THEE-ree-um)

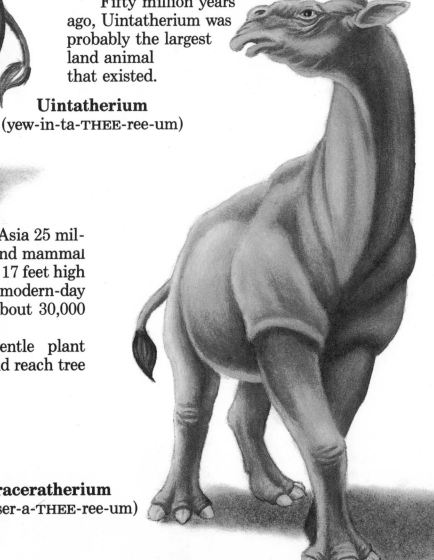

**Paraceratherium** lived in Asia 25 million years ago. It is the largest land mammal that has ever lived and was about 17 feet high at the shoulder. A relative of the modern-day rhinoceros, this giant weighed about 30,000 pounds.

Paraceratherium was a gentle plant eater. Using its long neck, it could reach tree branches 25 feet off the ground.

**Paraceratherium**
(par-a-ser-a-THEE-ree-um)

21

There were many different kinds of **saber-toothed cats.** Most were the size of tigers, only heavier and stronger. The largest cats had 9-inch-long fangs which helped make these animals very successful hunters. They first appeared about 30 million years ago and only died out about 10,000 years ago.

**Saber-Toothed Cat**

There were several types of **glyptodonts.** Some were 14 feet long and almost 5 feet high. Others were much smaller.

A relative of the armadillo, **Glyptodon** lived mostly in South America. Glyptodon ate insects, worms, and berries from the ground as it slowly moved along. The huge claws on its front feet were ideal for digging up roots and overturning rocks. Its strong tail sometimes had spikes on the end and was probably used to fend off enemies.

**Glyptodon**
(GLIP-toe-don)

# Megatherium
## (meg-uh-THEE-ree-um)

**Megatherium** was a giant South American ground sloth. Standing almost as tall as an elephant, the sloth spent its day feeding on leaves. Large claws helped it to pull down branches that grew above it.

Megatherium could not run, or even walk, very fast. When the giant sloth did move, it shuffled along on the sides of its feet. Megatherium had little to fear from most flesh eaters. On top of its skin were bony plates that were covered with thick, heavy hair. Even the saber-toothed cat would have trouble biting into this creature.

Megatherium died out only about 10,000 years ago, possibly hunted to extinction by early humans.

Several times during the last million years, large parts of the world were covered with ice. The **woolly mammoth** was protected from the cold by a thick layer of fat. In addition, this smallish elephant was covered with long, shaggy red-brown hair.

The mammoth's curved ivory tusks could be as long as 16 feet. Some scientists think the tusks were used to sweep away snow so the mammoth could find plants to eat.

A lot is known about the woolly mammoth. Some of their frozen bodies have been found in the ice of Siberia. One mammoth that died 12,000 years ago was found preserved in perfect condition. Its last meal was still in its stomach. It had eaten 30 pounds of pine needles, pinecones, flowers, and moss.

Primitive humans hunted the woolly mammoth for its flesh. At the end of the last ice age the climate became warmer and woolly mammoths died out.

The prehistoric animals are all gone now. But for many millions of years, they ruled the land, air, and sea.

**Woolly Mammoth**
(woo-lee MAM-uth)